Celebrate Christmas in the spring, sounds crazy, but here's the thing...
AF256436

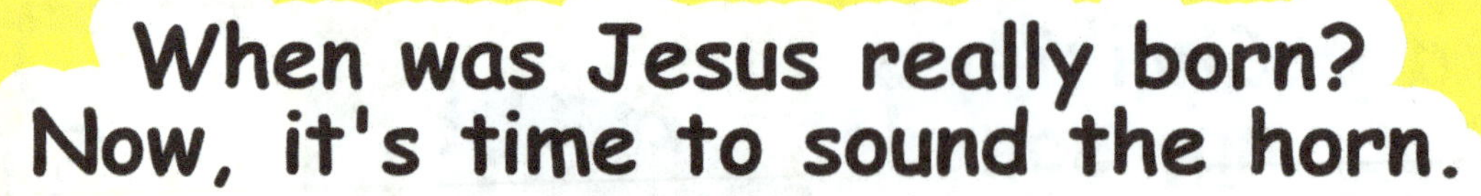

When was Jesus really born?
Now, it's time to sound the horn.

December, celebrated as the time,
Read on to find, how it's a crime.
Let's take a journey to the past,
To see signs that are vast.

Springtime is here,
One season a year.
Sleeping shepards in fields with their sheep,
Awaiting new lambs added to keep.

All lambs born this time of year,
For God, few worthy to bring near.
Best chosen to pay sin's price
for the Passover sacrafice.

Passover, the Jewish holiday
Hebrews freed from Egypt, yay!
Suffering and pain, under Pharoah's reign.
God freed the slave from his chain.

Sacrificing a lamb so pure,
Meant cleansed from sin, reassure.
That all changed the day Jesus came.
The Lamb of God born to reclaim


LAMB
LIVES
MATTER
BAAA!

You and me, now set free
The Lamb of God was the key.
No more lambs or sacrifices needed
Jesus paid, death defeated!

Far from over,
Jesus born and died on Passover.
That's in the month of Nisan,
Of the Hebrew calendar, moving on...
Not like the newer calendars of today,
God's calendar, based on moon, was here to stay.
APRIL
NISAN
1 2 3 4 5 6
7 8 9 10 11 12 13
14 15 16 17 18 19 20
21 22 23 24 25 26 27
28 29 30

Passover in the month of Nisan, what does this mean???
Let's read on before it gets too late, about Nisan and the Passover date...

Nisan, the start of the Hebrew calendar year,
Has a meaning that is very clear.
Nisan means The Beginning,
Which has all believers grinning.
Happy New Year!

Jesus died in the month of Nisan.
Jesus was raised in the month of Nisan.
BC became AD, the old calendar withdrew.
Not a mistake, Nisan means all things new!

Closer to knowing Jesus's birth date,
Here's the evidence you can't debate.
Keep track of these clues,
pieces of this puzzle are easy to confuse.

First day of Nisan, Nisan 1, was a Holy Day.
Holy days commanded men to Jerusalem, far away.
Although a Holy Day, Nisan 1 was not that way.
So Joseph and Mary were together that day.

Now we know Joseph was there with Mary,
In Bethlahem on that day, not the contrary.
The events unfolding as if designed with reason
Leading up to the greatest of season.

Remember the Hebrew calendar, how it's based on the Moon?
What this means, you'll find out soon.
Each month starts with a moon that's new,
By mid-month it's full to view.

The 14th of Nisan is Passover's date.
The day Jesus died to clear sin's slate.
Now we know the moon, too full to hide.
Now we know it was full when he died.

The beginning symbolized by a new moon in the sky,
It's fulfillment would be marked by a full moon up high.
Jesus, born on a moon that was new,
He died with a full moon in view.

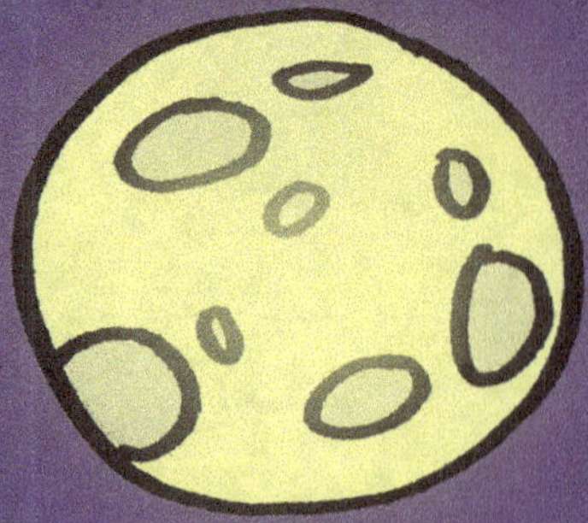

The Tabernacle is God's house, He dwels with us.
What God did next is impressive to discuss.
A pregnancy takes months, a total of nine.
The very same number to build this great shrine.

GOD'S CHOSEN DAY!
NISAN
1 2 3 4 5 6
7 8 9 10 11 12 13
28 29 30
TODO
Commmanded by God to be completed this day,
The Tabernacle was raised on time they say.
This day reapearing,
The day you keep hearing.
Nisan One,
with it's obvious relation to the Son.

Nisan 1, the day everything turns new,
Should really be the last clue.
If we consider these signs,
Jesus' birthday on Nisan 1 shines.

Now we know when Jesus was born,
Let us shoutout loud or sound a loud horn.
Finally solved the Holy of mysteries,
The news must be shared to correct false histories.

JESUS WAS BORN IN THE SPRING!
So how did the confusion become so great?
This news may come with some weight.
Never the less your burden to bare,
the truth about Christmas you're needed to share.

Even old Saint Nic who delivered the toys to all the girls and boys.
Gave to others as God's gift was the source of his joys.
Wanting to share Jesus and who He died for.
The price Christ paid, he said don't ignore.

DECEMBER
1 2 3 4 5 6 7
8 9 10 11 12 13 14
15 16 17 18 19 20 21
22 23 24 25 26 27 28
29 30 31
Without the best of motives, they moved Christmas' date.
Perhaps to get their church numbers to inflate.
For Pagans who were not looking for change,
Combining the Winter Solstice was not looking so strange.

Most symbols seen as we near this holiday,
Are actually from the old Pagan way.
Pine Trees, Mistletoe and Holly,
All Pagan practices, Oh gee-golly!

Now knowing this powerful truth,
What a blessing to learn early in youth.
When springtime rolls around,
Gather your family 'round.

HAPPY BIRTHDAY!
Double the presents for everyone,
When we celebrate Jesus' Birthday on Nisan One!
Not sure what Mom and Dad will say,
Eitherway Celebrate Christmas on the real Christmas Day!
Happy Birthday Jesus!
HAPPY B-DAY!!
HAPPY B-DAY!!
HAPPY B-DAY!!